The Player Queen's Wife

OLIVER REYNOLDS

The Player Queen's Wife

faber and faber
LONDON · BOSTON

First published in 1987
by Faber and Faber Limited
3 Queen Square London WC1N 3AU

Photoset by Wilmaset Birkenhead Wirral
Printed in Great Britain by
Richard Clay Ltd Bungay Suffolk

British Library Cataloguing in Publication Data

Reynolds, Oliver
The player queen's wife.
I. Title
821'.914   PR6068.E9/
ISBN 0–571–14998–7
ISBN 0–571–14999–5 (Pbk)

Acknowledgements

Icarus, Kontrast (Oslo), *London Magazine, London Review of Books, PN Review, Poetry Book Society Anthology 1986/7, Poetry Review, The Rialto, Spectator* and *Times Literary Supplement.*

I am grateful for the help, financial and otherwise, of a number of institutions:
  the Britten–Pears Foundation
  Hawthornden International Retreat for Writers
  the Judith E. Wilson Fund
  Darwin College
  the Eric Gregory Trust Fund

Contents

I

Rorschach Writing   3

II

Calvert's 'Chamber Idyll'   17
Words for Horatio   19
The Doctor   20
Three Rorschach Remnants   23
Theme and Variation   27
Thaw   28
The Player Queen's Wife   30

III

Seven little Sonnets on Frederick the Great   35
    The Prince   35
    The Pragmatist   35
    A Soldier Punished Twice   35
    Knapsack   36
    Map   36
    'On Playing the Flute'   36
    After Battle   37
This is his Coat   38
Works   40
Hazel   43
Brecht: A Worker Reads and Asks   45

IV

On Entering the Aviary   49
One would Think the Deep to be Hoary   50
From the Irish   52

Baudelaire's Pipe   54
Auden Hotel   55

V

Thirteen Days in a Northern City   63
Dispossessed   66
To Whom It May Concern   67
L.M.C. 1890   69
Tone Poem   71
  Eous   71
  Bestiary   72
  Phaethon   73
  Bless You!   74
  Woodsman   76
  Tone   77
  Maps   78

for Tone

I

I am! yet what I am who cares, or knows?

John Clare

Rorschach Writing

The large redbrick chapel,
set apart from the main building,
is used as a storehouse
for a number of surplus items
including:

70 pews (stacked on the altar),
104 iron-frame beds,
1 gross of coronation mugs,
30 tables,
19 copies of *Gray's Anatomy*,
14 wardrobes,
2 doz. white coats (mildewed),
80 yards of fire-hose
and 3 busts of Queen Victoria.

Only one door is in use.
Some of its keys are missing
and there are often signs
of unauthorized entry
including:

2 half-eaten Eccles cakes
and 1 used condom (Fetherlite)
in one of the wardrobes

and, throughout the building,
pages torn from an E3a logbook
and filled by a treatise
closely written in pencil,

'On the Indoor Use of Umbrellas:
studies in superstition,
hubris and user-fatality'.

2

Fat spatters counterpoint
to Cook's rock-bottom hum.

She shovels the pan across flame
and sixty sausages bump and nuzzle.

I sit in a room placid with mirrors
using a 2B at a round table
whose floor-length cloth tents my knees.
A small box rests on the paper,
brass rods framing glass
and a mirror, face up, at the bottom.
It seems that the leaves
patterning the glass lid
are also engraved on the mirror
till you lift the lid
and the two patterns diverge into one
leaving you your face clear in your hands.

Through the window I can see chimney-stacks,
sandstone drying and lightening after rain.
Through the door open on to the lawn
come the sound of peacocks rending air
and the river's insinuative sigh.

There is no river.
No window, no table, no box.
The door is locked.

Till a key in the lock
brings the floor-mop smell of cabbage.

She wears a yellow uniform
relieved by white at cap and belt.
On the left breast
a watch handstands at noon.

She carries a case and a paper bag.
In the case is a jacket
with buckles at the shoulders
and strangely long sleeves
which have no openings for the hands
but end in leather straps.

In the paper bag are two Eccles cakes.

Is it because the sleeves are so long
that Mr Prout's hands cannot be seen?

Or is it because his cricket-jumper,
besides Mr Prout, also contains Miss Peel?

Mr Prout and Miss Peel, wicket-keeper
and first slip (irrespectively),

are making notes on paper
torn from an E3a logbook:

'Time Freud's symbolical wheels were spoked –
an umbrella is an umbrella is an umbrella.'

Blue crams the sky.
The umpires sing.

The batsman aims for the chapel.
The ball recedes, hangs and returns.

Four hands thrust from the jumper
and bloom into a bowl.

With nowhere else to go,
the ball submits as the clapping starts.

I was Craven Arms, I was.
I was Craven Arms.
Stencilling the makes of wagon.
Named after fish.
Craven Arms main siding.
WHALE, SHARK and SALMON.
Stencilled in white.
Stencilling.

And the wheeltappers.
Tap. Tap.
Wheeltapping.
Sticks of chalk they had.
For tonnages and messages.
'Away' 'Away' always circled.
Chalk all grimy.
Tap. Tap.
'Away'.

Though fanciful, setting watches by him
would be reasonably accurate.

He makes two circuits of the grounds daily:
the morning and afternoon run.

His nose dribbles clots of stubble;
he has the usual high-shaved nape.

A green shirt-tail flaps like a signal-flag;
bustling shoulders wrench the buttoned jacket.

The home stretch is up the drive,
hard-going for a fifty-year-old.

His fists, tight on twelve-inch rulers,
strain and gather, piston-punching.

Spittle bubbles on his chin
as he chuffs and chuffs.

He is thickset, sweaty and frowning.
He is fast. He is unstoppable.

8

There are two wings
built around a horseshoe of corridor
just wide enough to allow
electric tugs meeting one another
to pass by slowly, their trailers
(loaded with milk-crates or laundry)
scraping and clicking.

Twelve doors, numbered 1 to 3,
are lettered 'E' or 'W'
for east or west wing
and 'a' or 'b'
for ground or first floor.

Each has a small glassed panel
with a brass indicator showing
(both inside and out)
whether the door is locked or free.
This enables anticipation,
especially useful
when the hands are full.

The doorknobs are brass
and do not turn.

9

After two injections
(anaesthetic and muscle-relaxant),
a rubber grip's inserted in the mouth
wedging the teeth;
the temples are then dabbed with paste,
electrodes attached
(trailing wire back
to the small varnished wood box)
and the switch turned.

The body seizes;
mechanical, it overloads.
The scrunched face is centripetal
and the shot forehead
snaking with live-wire veins.
The wishbone spine strains
and the limbs hammer.

When it's over,
the body is turned on one side,
dead weight
as if just thrown through a wall,
and wheeled next-door
where curtains are drawn round,
briskly, on shushing rings.

My coverlet over me,
blue top, white underside,
that Hokusai wave.

The headlice dream.
But not lice:
small scrunchy bodies
shower into the sink.

Coverlet heaped on my head.
Counterpain.

Making waves.
'Whelmed in deeper gulfs'.
In my father's copy
the man drowning
behind tissue paper,
one hand held up
to the speck of ship.
'Whelmed in deeper'.
Your finger lifted
and the tissue paper
curling back on him,
a thin rustle
blurring him.

Beyond the chapel,
high firs are clotted with nests.

Resting sheer on stiff wings
like oars paused in water, crows flock over

or muscle upward,
black blazonry jagged on sky.

Two axe down to plump on the aerial
above the TV room.

They break vowels on the roof
then, together, thump off.

Inside, the six o'clock news
breaks into chevrons.

A minute later,
the aerial is still trembling.

Bulbs burst yellow
over the walls' glared paint.
The corridor curves and diminishes,
a comet-tail glitter trailing the tug
just passed with its load of laundry
(dirty washing in the white bags,
soiled in the blue).

The corridor's boxed with brightness.
There is a smell of tired disinfectant,
a sixty-watt silence.
Night glasses blank windows.
Doorknobs bend a dotted line
to its vanishing-point,
brass winks relayed through unused air.

II

I have spent the whole day on urgent matters. The battle plan is complete. So I think I'm just as entitled as the next man to knock off some verses.

Frederick II

Calvert's 'Chamber Idyll'

With this first line
the body's subsumed
into the Empire of the Eye.

The real room recedes
till there's only
the room you're making.

Found, objects
tell themselves
to scorper and burin:

fruit, rope,
planks in perspective,
a sickle.

Graining a roof-beam,
you draw wood
from the wood;

stippling skin,
you gouge
narrative.

Unimpressed,
a bull watches
sheep seethe

from its horns'
rhetorical
questions.

A plough's capsized
on the horizon.
The sky

unsheaves
its harvests.
Three soft stars flare.

Words for Horatio

I would have named a son after him,
but we only had girls.
It might have been an exorcism,
a ridding of the half-life left to me
when he hugged death to himself –
'Selfish to the end.' That's the wife's view,
but she was sick of it all long ago.

They recently tried a murderer, son of a Norwegian,
who'd killed fifteen times, stashing bodies
about his rooms like lumber,
then cutting them up, boiling down heads
in a saucepan on the stove,
his top window wide open through the winter.

One all-but-corpse, doped and half-strangled,
had been let off and warmed back to life.
He'd remembered little in the morning
and been shocked by his neck, zippered with red.
At the trial, though, he'd relived his near-death
and since then, in a voice grated raw with weeping,
he's lamented his fag-end of a life,
lamented his exclusion from death.

Twenty years ago, the thrash of events
compelled me to goodness. Disinterring,
year by year, I poke for motivations.
They shred in my fingers.
All that's left is the explication of bone.

The Doctor

He was married
and had his first posting
within a fortnight.

They spent the honeymoon
looking for rooms on the outskirts
of a crumbling Empire

and moving furniture
with the help of an old man
and a donkey.

The army was pulling out.
It was a period of curfews
and edginess, of fingers

on safety-catches.
Two soldiers beat up a barman
so badly, he died.

They were condemned to hang.
The doctor was detailed
to attend them in the cells.

(He was also told
that after the execution
he would sign the certificates.)

One soldier, McCullen,
came from a village ten miles
from the doctor's home town.

They talked about fishing –
pools and streams
miles and years away.

The hanging was at dawn.
As McCullen lifted his head
for the rope, he revealed

a jaw-line strung
with the dried blood
of shaving-cuts.

The night before,
the doctor had asked him
if he wanted

any sleeping-pills.
'Ask me tomorrow, Doc.
Ask me tomorrow.'

Twenty years on, now a GP,
he couldn't forget
that fortnight of cell visits.

Worried obsessively
in bars and clubs,
his memory suppurated.

His drinking became chronic.
He kept a bottle
in his visiting-bag.

The night he died,
he couldn't sleep
and sat up drinking.

When his wife
suggested a Valium,
he shook his head.

'Ask me tomorrow, dear.
Ask me tomorrow.'

Three Rorschach Remnants

The old incinerator rusts,
its name-plate (*FAIRFAX*, *Lancs.*)
heat-bent and crazing.

It was served by a flue
ending in a stub of chimney
next to the tower's domed roof
over a hundred feet up.

Under the dome is a gallery
with a clear view of the grounds:
a rough circle sometimes split
by the tower's bar of shadow
stalled across it like an hour hand.

In it gushes, the Samaritan bore,
broaching the gates to rill the corridors
whiles I make steady watch, resisting rock
buffeted by the Sam twins, Flot and Jet.

In for an afternoon
of tea and sympathy
chat and biscuits
such good listeners
or would you like a walk
out on the grass, dear,
down by the trees.

Elms vail and saunter under brooding wind.

Or back to the canteen
sarsaparilla and a sandwich.

Whiles I stand and watch the corridor curve.

The new incinerator is gas-fired.
Once, having left the burners on,
I returned to find the steel sides
glowing and throbbing.
Cooled to a flaky ash-white,
their hurt bulge is permanent.

It's mostly domestic rubbish:
paper, toast crusts, peel, boxes.
Aerosols crump in the fire's gut
or explode by the open flap,
slicing out metal into the air.

Occasionally, there are records:
lists of names, dates, conditions –
bare histories going up in smoke.
Some old reports are leather-bound
with sharp-edged endpapers
sheened in marble or porphyry.
Many are only half-full.
Pages clog, unburnt, in the flames;
when separated by the iron raker
they show white before catching.

The lab sawdust burns slowly,
often wet and sour with piss
and strewn with pellets of shit.
The rats are flung in on Wednesdays,
inert bumps in a sack
sharp with formaldehyde.

I once found a litter
burrowed in a bin of sawdust.
Thumb-sized, purple and blind,
they had soft tip-snouts
and kept cheeping thinly.

Theme and Variation

Ludwig had perfect pitch
and whistled wonderfully,
placing notes as easily
as putting a hat on a peg.

Paul, his pianist brother,
lost an arm in World War I.
Ravel wrote him a concerto –
the one for Left Hand.

*

You hear very little now
of Roger Whittaker.
Maybe he's concentrating
on a *Tractatus* of his own.

Nice if he still had
something up his sleeve,
like Nelson
after Tenerife.

Thaw

It was a pure world, snow-covered.

I was working on an algebraic model
of the long fall, almost aleatory, of flakes
intersected by slicing and sweeping gulls
when the phone rang:

the Radio Committee boss going bazurkas
because the Friend of Children had tuned into
Yudina playing the Mozart 23rd
and wanted the record of it.
Who was the boss to say it was a live broadcast?
If the Great Gardener thought it was a record,
it was a record: if Stalin said shit,
you shat.

So off they went to Archives to find
Yudina had never recorded the 23rd.
We had to do it then. That night.

The studio was frigid bedlam;
the tympanist was still in his pyjamas,
the woodwind had no scores
so, out of habit, were falling back on the '1812'
while the conductor was so nervous
his adagio kept twitching into allegro.

Yudina was the only calm one;
when I swore at a fuse blowing she said
'You're far from God, you must be closer to God.'

We made the pressing at daybreak: just one copy.
Three of us took it over to Dispatch
like a bomb disposal squad with Parkinson's.
Snow huffed and puffed at us all the way;
it was 16 below and we were sweating.
Carrying it, I felt limp and giggly;
I remembered the Latin *effetus*:
weakened by having brought forth young.

That record was on the turntable in his dacha
when the Great Railway Engineer finally died:
the music at an end, allegro assai,
whirling outer air configured with flakes
and the still pause inside tightening
at 78 revolutions a minute
scrik . . . scrik . . . scrik . . . scrik . . .

The Player Queen's Wife

for Tone

Our stage was Europe,
dragging from country to country
in a cart sold off by a rain-broken farmer
and trusting to the company's seven languages
(Garbo, a Gypsy and our Fool, had four of them).

A life spent trailing a cart
or, pregnant again, bouncing inside it
on a mattress of dusty curtains;
a life of haggling with innkeepers;
of naming the yearly children
after old Gods and dead actors;
of days stalled by a river
waiting for it to go down,
brown water thrashing like an animal's back.

And then, having come through mountains
or reached the steepled horizon across the plain
or that castle up on its crags
where the creeping Jesus in black
told us our own job – with actions –
once we'd arrived and unpacked,
made our bargain and beaten our drum,
I'd watch a stubbly queen
make me presents of myself:

daydreaming, she'd stop half-way
through pulling up a stocking
(as I've done, thinking of home)
or, laughing, splay her fringe (the best wig)
with a gesture I've had since a girl
or finally, at the bows and curtsies,
she'd grin and lift her skirts
to show again the stockings
I thought I'd lost two towns ago.

III

Friedrich der Zweite siegte im Siebenjährigen Krieg.
Wer Siegte außer ihm?

Bertolt Brecht

Seven little Sonnets on Frederick the Great

The Prince

Fate forcing
a baby crown
over a sibling's head

left him christened
but dead.

The Pragmatist

Frederick
specialized
in disdain:

'The crown is a hat
that lets in the rain.'

A Soldier Punished Twice

'So,
using his horse
for bestiality . . .

Get him out of irons –
into the infantry.'

Knapsack

Spare breeches, shirts,
gaiter buttons and flints;
hair powder, mirror; cutlery;

bandage
and tourniquet.

Map

Austria versus
Prussia:
the Seven Years War

left Europe
like a cracked tile floor.

'On Playing the Flute'

Frederick II
practising *embouchure*
with Quantz

pursed his lips.
The master looked askance.

After Battle

Woodwind's dwindled away,
but air's
still drumming

with the stench
of what were men.

This is his Coat

A plain officer's coat
of Prussian blue
with red collar and cuffs

(which allowed any subaltern
to claim he wore
des Königs Rock),

the whole of the front
is powdered and smeared
with Spanish snuff.

The pockets are lined
with chamois leather
so as not to scratch

any of his collection
of fifteen hundred
jewelled snuff-boxes.

Unusually,
he wore his sword-sash
outside the coat

hoping the sash and sword
would mask his odd shape –
the wide hips and hollow back.

He felt the cold
and buttoned the lapels
across his chest

which also helped to secure
the dog he often rode with
snug under his chin.

(Greyhounds were his favourite
and he built graves for them
on the terrace at Sans Souci.)

His love of dogs
was shared by a later leader:
Hitler, saying that only Eva Braun

and Blondi were faithful to him,
would quote Frederick's remark:
'Now I know men, I prefer dogs.'

Works

Staying at Sans Souci, Voltaire
went over Frederick's poetry for him –

he called this
'washing the king's dirty linen'.

The prose was more self-reliant,
as is shown by just one title

from the thirty-volume *Œuvres*
(he wrote – and fought – in French):

Instructions Militaires
du Roi de Prusse pour ses Généraux.

*

In the Seven Years War
the Jung-Braunschweig regiment lost

1,650 men
through desertion.

So,
guard your troops.

Give them beer.
Put sentries in the cornfields.

Never camp near a forest.
Never march at night.

The portable field oven can bake
1,000 6lb. loaves daily.

Though biscuits take up less pack-space
than bread, they're not so sustaining

as the men mix them with water
and drink them as soup.

Firewood should always be made up of logs:
we forbid the practice

of setting alight
the houses of the peasantry.

*

The army is built
on discipline –

or, more exactly,
on fear.

The common soldier
should fear his officer

more than the enemy:
the horse prospers

under the eye
of its master.

*

Know the land. Talk to old inhabitants,
especially shepherds and gamekeepers.

Before battle, go to the nearest height,
map in hand, and study the view.

Cemeteries and sunken roads
make excellent defensive positions.

Know the land. What if that marsh
covering your flank

turns out to be a dry field?
What if that river freezes over?

Hazel

Take two hundred soldiers.
Form into two ranks facing each other
at a distance of six to seven feet.

Each man has a rod of hazel,
soaked in water, a yard long
and about three-quarters of an inch thick.

The offender is stripped to the waist
and his hands tied in front of him.
He is made to walk between the ranks.

(A sergeant precedes him, walking backwards
with a pike levelled at his chest,
to dissuade him from trying to run.)

Pipes and drums play throughout.
Each soldier gives the offender
one blow on his bare back.

Corporals with staves should be ready
to beat any soldier
not exerting himself.

Depending on the severity of the offence,
the gauntlet is to be run
twelve, twenty-four or thirty-six times.

Those undergoing it thirty-six times
(spread over three days)
usually die.

Blood-loss may so exhaust the offender
(the back will be flayed and strips of skin
often hang down over the breeches)

that he collapses: he should receive
the remaining blows lying down,
the soldiers marching past him in file.

Brecht: A Worker Reads and Asks

for Dave Griffiths

Who built Thebes with its seven gates?
Books say it was kings.
Did kings hew and haul the rock?
And Babylon razed again and again,
who rebuilt it again and again? Where
in gilded Lima did the builders live?
When the Great Wall of China was finished
and it was evening, where did the masons go?
Monuments commemorate Roman victories. Who
carved them? Who lost when the Caesars won?
Did the Byzantines live only in palaces
and poems? Even when Atlantis sank
into myth, the sea had to drown
men howling for their slaves.

The young Alexander conquered India.
On his own?
Caesar smote the Gauls.
Wasn't there at least a cook with him?
Philip of Spain wept when his armada
went to the bottom. Did no one else weep?
Frederick the Great won the Seven Years War. Who
won beside him?

A victory per page.
Who cooked the victory feast?
A great man per decade.
Who paid the bill?

So much to read.
So much to ask.

IV

. . . he became his admirers.

W. H. Auden

On Entering the Aviary

The sheaney's call is distinctive
as is the brilliance of its plumage.

The craine is exotic enough
to have come from another planet.

Though the plarkin
is of a great and wry beauty,

the roost is ruled
by thughes.

As well as these *Fabbaf* species,
there are many others

from the Nile-wader
or beguiling shill

to the fowls of Eire feasting
on young shoots of sbarry-grass.

Awkward fledgling,
I flap to a perch

between the rare jormond
and the migrating dabse.

One would Think the Deep to be Hoary

for Sebastian Barry

Possible seals disappearing
far out off Pembrokeshire,
sleek commas suddenly lost
in the sea's murky prose,

came back to me (memories
taking a year to surface)
as we returned at midnight
from the Laird and Dog.

It was our daily goal,
two poets retreating
from a Writers' Retreat
to beer's bitter salve.

We'd walk out at twilight
up a drive squeezed through firs
shuttled over by crows
readying for the night

(or once, flung from their nests,
fissile, by a donkey's blaring
Bronx roars through Midlothian
in fractured Trombonese)

and return, talking poetry
in the half-seas-over dark,
down the drive's black on black
curving into deeper dark.

And from poetry, to language:
the world flitched and hung up
in all the different words
in all the different tongues.

Beneath firs weighed by sleeping crows
seal was named in Gaelic –
madra na mara,
the dog of the sea,

while the Welsh one waited,
forgotten and sunk
in the dictionary –
morlo, forlorn *morlo*

only remaining as an image,
greys glint-slicked on distance
and then reclaimed by the sea
bulking in from Ireland.

Seeing them dive again,
ripples bodied through water,
I wondered if they could hear
those unfathomable sounds

of our juke-box favourite,
'Memphis, Tennessee', when Chuck Berry
stretches a guitar string to boom
solid echoes like whales courting.

From the Irish

There's a head by Blake
with wingspan eyebrows
of a man who taught him
'Painting &c
in his Dreams'.

Waking now like Jonah
in a room ribbed with dark
I find your face persists,
a fearful smeared grey
crying success and failure.

My throat cracks,
the mouth struck open
on hollowed breathing:
dumb gusts
in the small cave.

Last Ash Wednesday
we read together in Dublin
in Buswell's downstairs bar,
our table and chairs
backdropped by a door

marked GENTLEMEN
and our poems saluted
at quarter-hour intervals
by the urinals
sputtering applause.

Off the airport bus
by the bookshop (a Kavanagh
first edition for 60 punts)
and the kids begging silver
on the Halfpenny Bridge,

I'd seen two men
with soft cindery moles
on their foreheads.
Coincidence, I'd thought.
Or brothers.

Baudelaire's Pipe

I am the pipe of a writer.
The Asian tints congealed
inside my bowl reveal
my master's a heavy smoker.

I'm busiest, a small hookah
bubbling with zeal,
when he's down and he feels
life's dealt him the Joker.

I puff balm,
hazing haloes
of shifting blues

till he's calm,
having taken his cure
from pungent air.

Auden Hotel

for Edward Carr and Ruth Hutton

I

Slats of rain slap the street;
rain boils over concrete;
gutters well; the road's camber
succumbs to water.

A taxi docks at the kerb.
Unprotected and unperturbed,
a fat man levers himself out and stands
looking up at a hotel sign, his hands

incarnadined as his jumper-sleeves run.
The sign fizzes: 'Hotel . . . Hotel . . . Auden . . .'
The man grunts and then, like a tidal bore,
bursts the hotel's revolving door.

II

Just back, I'm glad to say, from Rio,
the Hotel Trio
is lost in the K563
(the healthiest highs come musically).

A forehead drips perspiration.
The cello's huge hesitation,
throbbed from its palm-court oasis,
shivers empty glasses.

A girl reading Leconte de Lisle
hums between bites of veal.
The music uncoils to a close.
The musicians pause, then rosin their bows.

III

Three in the morning:
the night porter, sallow and yawning,
sets out greasy cards for patience.
The lift-bell pings. (In the suspense

before the doors rumble back,
the Queen's covered by the Jack.)
It's empty – but for scattered pills,
a pair of tights and some handbills:

INTERNATIONAL POETRY SEMINAR
1st Meeting at 9.00 in the Limestone Bar
P. Rathbone: What I Owe to Yeats
The porter sweeps them up, then spits.

IV

Washed-out dawn
and a ghost crumples on the hotel lawn:
a nightshirt, and on it a lipstick smear:
'Nationalize Earl's Court Square.'

Rathbone walks shoe-lined corridors.
'These shoes were left by their owners,
saints making a sudden Ascension . . .
or is that too Martian?'

The dreams of poets are destroyed
by the hissing of the Teasmaid.
Downstairs, there's egg or kipper,
each plate flanked by pen and paper.

V

'Well, she's more *TLS* than *LRB*:
attractive, but formal. More tea?'
'Good morning. I'm Wu. From Taiwan.
Ranslator. My main incest is Byron.'

'. . . like trying to lasso a tank.
All political poetry is wank.'
'When did Selima marry Geoffrey?'
'My Theory of Metre, briefly . . .'

Cigarette smoke palls the din.
11 o'clock. The waiters begin
clearing ash-strewn plates.
Rathbone's still rabbiting on about Yeats.

VI

What keeps them going:
egos with more thrust than a Boeing
or just a verbal itch
that they have to scratch?

What'll we remember when they're dead?
A maid strips a bed
and finds (impossible at the Hilton)
a Durex bookmarking Milton.

[57]

Why do poets piss in the sink –
is it all that drink?
Why is so much they write plain bad?
And why do so many go mad?

VII

Sunday afternoon thickens.
Whiffs of roast chicken
infiltrate a cubby-hole
where, happy as a bacchanal,

I lift my tea-cup.
Someone turns a radio up
for a programme on La Fontaine's *Fables*.
I rest slippered feet on the table;

minutes later,
lulled by the thudding dumb-waiter,
Times crossword abandoned to the Muses,
Mr Auden, Proprietor, snoozes.

VIII

The last poet drives off,
leaving a sonnet and forgetting a glove.
The newest guests write their names in the book:
'Mr and Mrs Smith, Porlock'.

The air's growing cooler.
Foolscap feeds the boiler
(Rathbone's efforts and illusions).
Curtains are drawn, like conclusions.

Because our words outlive our acts,
listen to cadences, not facts.
Finale time, these words show it:
trust the poem, not the poet.

V

O timbers from Norway and muscles from Wales . . .

Idris Davies

Thirteen Days in a Northern City

The world inflates with light.
Statues take shape in the park:
a man balances babies on his foot,
a foetus stands on its head.

Gates are unlocked.
A fountain shudders into life.
An early tram scythes by
on a kiss of metal.

Grass has grown thick
between the tracks
and the tram slips downhill
as if released into a field.

*

A wide curtainless room
jiggles with sun;
empty wine-bottles
fume with light.

There's a sharp twitter
of swifts in the street.
Shadows blurt across the window.
The carpet's covered

with trousers in précis
and the semaphore of shirts.
In your bed, we sleep tighter
than fossils in stone.

The palace is a simple cube
painted a calm orange
and topped by a TV aerial.
There is a lone sentry.

Like most people, the King
goes to the mountains to ski,
normally driving, but when cars
were banned during the Oil Crisis

he took a tram for the first time.
At the door, loaded with skis,
he asked the conductor:
'Do I have to pay?'

*

The island has a clear view
of the ski-jump
perched above the city
like a huge knife-rest.

Tonsures and shaved heads:
there was once a monastery here
and a prison-camp after the war
for women who'd had German lovers.

We lie at the water's edge.
A speedboat slaps over swell.
You doze and I sip and sip
at the warmth of your neck.

*

Night pools around the candles.
Eating shrimps bought at the quay,
the smell on our fingers
turns from marine to nocturnal.

Dispossessed

Gathered hills bring the sky closer,
stoppering the valley with blue.

Tree ranks on the grassed tips
confuse the sun, corrugating shadow

to display Welsh Office economics:
ten thousand firs for every job.

Yellow bulldozers above Pontygwaith
huff black smoke, sculpting spoil.

Shade-torn light in the main street
suffers the sun's apartheid

and sold-up shops lead to the wreck
of a brewery: *Fernvale – Prince of Ales.*

Starlings congregate on empty chapels
to gloss and bicker the daily lesson.

To Whom It May Concern

In strictly economic terms it could be said the valleys
no longer have a reason for existing.
Welsh Office Report

Dear Jones/Jenkins/Rees/Roberts
(delete whichever is inapplicable)
as your Secretary of State
let me fill you in on your future:

you don't have one
(not if you stay where you are).
Sorry not to beat about the bush,
but that's Economics for you.

The last few jobs will soon be gone:
women making tellies for the Nips and men
taking tourists round the mining museums
(ex-NUM members need not apply).

So it's the dole for the rest of you.
But I don't want you to think
we'll be shelling it out for ever.
After all, this is Government, not Oxfam.

No, what's needed is some initiative,
some oomph, some get-up-and-go.
Well, we'll take care of the initiative
just so long as you get up and go.

(Anyway, who wants to stay in the Rhondda
with its 30% of pensioner households
without inside toilets – I mean
who'd be old with piles *and* chilblains?)

The obvious answer to all this
is something that combines
maximum security for your future
with investment on a large scale.

Led astray by red rabble-rousing,
you might think this Government
would never offer such a thing.
Well, you'd be wrong. We would and we do.

We have endeavoured, at great expense,
to find an area rich in those qualities
recognized as quintessentially Welsh:
lots of rain and lots of sheep.

Sufferers from *hiraeth* (I trust that's right)
needn't fret: Patagonia's just hours away
and there are echoes of home in your Islands'
new name – Falkland Fawr and Falkland Fach.

L.M.C. 1890

Crossing river, road and railway,
I pass the insistent notices:
'This bridge will be closed
if vandalism continues. NCB.'
Beyond the fence,
hundredweight chunks of motor
litter oil-caked earth
as if dropped during a robbery.

On this side of the valley
there are tables in the street,
flutters of bunting
and children eating and playing
to celebrate forty years
of Victory in Europe.
The kids play touch:
'On it. On it. Steve's on it.'

Dead ahead are the two wheels,
one stubborn with green paint
and the other rust-brown
with its cable running
uselessly tight
to the engine-house.
I remember the far wall
and the colliery initials
chiselled high up
above the opening date.
Five more years, I saw,
to another anniversary.

Walking back from Trehafod,
I found a small piece of coal
on the pavement
and it's now on my table:
an inch of memento,
a fossil's miniature strata
smattered with light.

I wonder if I'll still have it
in five years' time
and if I'll remember those kids
running down from the street
to the grassed-over tip
in their toy bowler hats:
plastic crowns brightly coloured
with slices of Union Jack.

Tone Poem

Eous

'Undress me! Undress me!' you said
dancing with your arms out like wings,
tiddly and giggly till you flopped over me:
'Undress me.'

I wound my hand
into the end of the belt
hanging down by your side:
'Just like a tail.'

In bed my fingers planed down soft
on soft of thigh and calf
till they came to your heel's roughness,
hard as the beginnings of a hoof.

Bestiary

Python-coils of leg and trunk
confuse the hand:
where do I stop and you begin?

That thumb-size hare
we saw in the Egyptian Gallery
had your stretched-back neck now

but not these fingers
grazing and ruminating
all over my back.

You bird-burr my name
then pigeon-pout oohs and ahs
as I grunt and root deeper.

Flopped apart,
flounders washed up
on the slab of the bed,

we gape at our groins
fresh-sprigged with dark parsley
and remember

how earlier that night
we kissed in a church doorway
as fire-engines whooped by

their lights flocking over us
the sudden flits and blues
of passerine and paradise.

Phaethon

The morning before the airport
I gave you my grey leather jacket
to be worn against Oslo's cold
and for remembrance
(Ophelia's rosemary turned sartorial),
my sleeves' surrogate arms holding
what I can only think of.

The night before the airport
I gave you a bruise on the upper arm,
passion setting a bleary sun
against the skin's white.
Your first letter tells me it's fading.
Counting the days to your return,
I run sunrise into sunrise.

Bless You!

That first day
we sat and talked by the river
watching ducks trawl

their ends of alphabets
across slick water
till we were interrupted

by a horse looming
through the gateway behind us
clacking hooves on stone

to stand gravely considering us
through the mist-wraiths
plumed from its nostrils.

We didn't touch then,
but a fortnight later
were kissing in the BM

before the bulged eyes
of an Elgin Marble horse-head,
stone strained and tendoned with effort,

your hand pocketing itself on my bum
as your tongue slid its slalom
through my lips and teeth.

Explaining how the Marbles
were another chunk of British booty,
I'd remembered you saying how

English itself had suffered other empires,
some of the words we use daily
having invaded the language from Norse.

Now back home, you ski or press
small capable fingers down the spine
of a volume of Kierkegaard

while I, colonized
by memory's imperium,
can only think

of your odd way of sneezing:
that equine half-cough
jerking your hair into a mane.

Woodsman

Passing two poplars, sombre and quiet
in a windless winter, I think of you
and your sister (unhappy in Bergen)
wrinkling into bark,
your arms branching into leaves
as you weep and weep amber.

I'll see you next in the spring
when your hair, lightening even further,
will blaze into blonde

and when these two poplars,
prosaic Heliades bogged in a fen
as scratching-posts for mist-huffing cattle,
will put on their yellows and greens
and recall other times
rustling and shimmering.

Tone

Your dodo surname,
you and your sister
being the last to bear it,
was a doddle to say

but your first name's Nordic
shibboleth was unjumpable:
when I introduced you to friends
hoofed poles clattered in my ears

so you had me anglicize it
to this abbreviated abbreviation
thus losing the native ring it has
as Thor's female equivalent

who I see as Thunder Woman
on a quiet cloudless day
domesticating her hammer
to put in a little farrier-work.

Maps

Just twenty, you went as a teacher
to an island beyond Hammerfest:

a flat-earther's dream
at the edge of the atlas,

a plume of land
nodding towards Russia

where, on a neat ocean
netted by meridians

and trawled by the Arctic Circle,
my finger finally traces you.

Here you had a house to yourself
hung between white dawn and sea:

endless day and a midnight sun
as heaven worked overtime

as it does now
in the morning constellations

found by my fingers mapping
your back's scatter of small moles.